Afghan Variegations™

General Information

Many of the products used in this pattern book can be purchased from local craft, fabric and variety stores, or from the Annie's Attic Needlecraft Catalog (see Customer Service information on page 16).

Contents

Watercolor
Ribbons

SKILL LEVEL

EASY

FINISHED SIZE
46 x 60½ inches

MATERIALS
- Red Heart Super Saver medium (worsted) weight yarn (solid: 7 oz/ 364 yds/198g per skein; multi: 5 oz/ 244 yds/141g per skein):
  8 skeins #310 Monet print
  2 skeins #528 medium purple
- Size I/9/5.5mm crochet hook or size needed to obtain gauge

4 MEDIUM

GAUGE
3 sc = 1 inch; 2 dc rows and 2 sc rows = 2 inches

PATTERN NOTE
Chain-3 at beginning of rows counts as first double crochet unless otherwise stated.

SPECIAL STITCH
Cross-stitch (cross-st): Skip next 2 sts **or** sk next dc and ch sp, dc in next st, ch 1, working in front of last dc made, dc in first sk st.

INSTRUCTIONS
AFGHAN
Row 1: With medium purple, ch 183, sc in 2nd ch from hook and in each ch across, turn. *(182 sc)*

Row 2: Ch 3 *(see Pattern Note)*, dc in next st, [**cross-st** *(see Special Stitch)*, dc in each of next 2 sts] across, turn. *(74 dc, 36 cross-sts)*

Row 3: Ch 3, dc in next st, [cross-st, dc in each of next 2 sts] across, turn.

Row 4: Ch 1, sc in each st and in each ch sp across, turn. Fasten off. *(182 sc)*

Row 5: Join Monet print with sc in first st, sc in next st, [ch 6, sk next 3 sts, sc in each of next 2 sts] across, turn. *(74 sc, 36 ch sps)*

Row 6: Ch 3, dc in next st, [ch 4, sk next ch sp, dc in each of next 2 sts] across, turn.

Row 7: Ch 3, dc in next st, [ch 3, sc around next 2 ch sps from last 2 rows at same time, ch 3, dc in each of next 2 sts] across, turn. *(74 dc, 72 ch sps, 36 sc)*

Row 8: Ch 1, sc in each of first 2 sts, [ch 3, sc in each of next 2 dc] across, turn. *(74 sc, 36 ch sps)*

Row 9: Ch 1, sc in each st and 3 sc in each ch sp across, turn. *(182 sc)*

Row 10: Ch 1, sc in each st across, turn.

Rows 11–14: Rep rows 5–8. Fasten off at end of last row.

Row 15: Join medium purple with sc in first st, sc in each st and 3 sc in each ch sp across, turn. *(182 sc)*

Rows 16–99: [Rep rows 2–15 consecutively] 6 times.

Rows 100–102: Rep rows 2–4. Fasten off at end of last row. ■

Dark
Harbor

SKILL LEVEL

◑■☐▭
EASY

FINISHED SIZE
44 x 57 inches

MATERIALS
- Red Heart Super Saver medium (worsted) weight yarn (solid: 7 oz/ 364 yds/198g per skein; multi: 5 oz/244 yds/141g per skein):
  9 skeins #794 bay print
  1 skein #341 light grey
- Size J/10/6mm crochet hook or size needed to obtain gauge

GAUGE
3 dc rows and 3 bphdc rows = 3 inches

PATTERN NOTE
Chain-3 at beginning of rows counts as first double crochet unless otherwise stated.

INSTRUCTIONS
AFGHAN
Row 1: With light grey, ch 173, dc in 4th ch from hook and in each ch across, turn. *(171 dc)*

Row 2: Ch 1, sc in first st, **bphdc** *(see Stitch Guide)* around each st across to last st, sc in last st, turn. Fasten off. *(169 bphdc, 2 sc)*

Row 3: Join bay print with sl st in first st, **ch 3** *(see Pattern Note)*, 4 dc in same st, *[dc in next st, sk next st] 8 times, dc in next st, 5 dc in each of next 2 sts, rep from * 7 times, [dc in next st, sk next st] 8 times, dc in next st, 5 dc in last st, turn. *(171 dc)*

Row 4: Ch 1, sc in first st, bphdc around each st across to last st, sc in last st, turn. *(169 bphdc, 2 sc)*

Rows 5–12: [Rep rows 3 and 4 alternately] 4 times. Fasten off at end of last row.

Row 13: Join light grey with sl st in first st, ch 3, dc in each st across, turn.

Rows 14–109: [Rep rows 2–13 consecutively] 8 times. Fasten off at end of last row. ■

Sea Shells

SKILL LEVEL

EASY

FINISHED SIZE
53 x 60 inches

MATERIALS
- Red Heart Super Saver medium (worsted) weight yarn (solid: 7 oz/ 364 yds/198g per skein; multi: 5 oz/244 yds/141g per skein):
  9 skeins #995 ocean
  1 skein #579 pale plum
- Size I/9/5.5mm crochet hook or size needed to obtain gauge

GAUGE
2 (9-dc) groups and 1 ch sp = 6 inches; 3 shell rows and 2 sc rows = 3½ inches

PATTERN NOTE
Chain-3 at beginning of rows counts as first double crochet unless otherwise stated.

SPECIAL STITCHES
Shell: (Dc, {ch 1, dc} 4 times) in indicated place.

Cluster (cl): Yo, insert hook in indicted ch sp, yo, pull lp through, yo, pull through 2 lps on hook, yo, insert hook in same sp, yo, pull lp through, yo, pull through 2 lps on hook, yo, pull through all 3 lps on hook.

INSTRUCTIONS
AFGHAN
Row 1: With ocean, ch 139 loosely, sc in 4th ch from hook *(first 3 chs count as first hdc and ch-1 sp)*, [sk next 3 chs, **shell** *(see Special Stitches)* in next ch, sk next 3 chs, sc in next ch, ch 3, sc in next ch] across to last 9 chs, sk next 3 chs, shell in next ch, sk next 3 chs, sc in next ch, ch 1, hdc in last ch, turn. *(15 shells)*

Row 2: **Ch 3** *(see Pattern Note)*, 2 dc in first ch-1 sp, [sk next ch sp, sc in next ch sp, ch 3, sc in next ch sp, 9 dc in next ch-3 sp] across to last 5 ch sps, sk next ch sp, sc in next ch sp, ch 3, sc in next ch sp, 3 dc in last ch sp, turn. *(14 9-dc groups)*

Row 3: Ch 3 *(counts as first hdc and ch-1 sp)*, sc in next st, [shell in next ch-3 sp, sk next 3 sts of next 9-dc group, sc in next st, ch 3, sk next st, sc in next st] across to last ch-3 sp, shell in last ch-3 sp, sk next dc, sc in next st, ch 1, hdc in last st, turn. *(15 shells)*

Rows 4–77: [Rep rows 2 and 3 alternately] 37 times.

BORDER
Rnd 1: Ch 1, 3 sc in first st, evenly sp 133 sc across each short end and 149 sc across each long edge around with 3 sc in each corner, join with sl st in beg sc. Fasten off. *(135 sc on each short end between center corner sts, 151 sc on each long edge between center corner sts)*

Rnd 2: Join pale plum with sl st in any st, ch 3 *(see Pattern Note)*, dc in each st around with 5 sc in each center corner st, join with sl st in 3rd ch of beg ch-3. *(139 dc on each short end between center corner sts, 155 dc on each long edge between center corner sts)*

Rnd 3: Join ocean with sc in any st, sc in each st around with 3 sc in each center corner st, join with sl st in beg sc. Fasten off. *(141 sc across each short end between center corner sts, 157 sc on each long edge between center corner sts)*

Rnds 4 & 5: Rep rnds 2 and 3. *(147 sc on each short end between center corner sts, 163 sc on each long edge between center corner sts at end of last rnd)*

Rnd 6: Join ocean with sl st in any center corner st before 1 short end, ch 4 *(counts as first dc and*

ch-1 sp), (dc, {ch 1, dc} 3 times) in same st, *sk next st, sc in next st, [sk next 3 sts, shell in next st, sk next 3 sts, sc in next st] across to one st before next center corner st, sk next st**, shell in next corner st, rep from * around, ending last rep at **, join with sl st in 3rd ch of beg ch-4. (80 shells)

Rnd 7: (Sl st, ch 2, dc) in first ch sp, [ch 3, **cl** (see Special Stitches) in next ch sp] 3 times, *cl in next ch sp, [ch 3, cl in next ch sp] 3 times, rep from * around, sk first ch-2 sp, join with sl st in beg dc. Fasten off. ■

Shades of
Autumn

SKILL LEVEL

BEGINNER

FINISHED SIZE
44 x 55 inches

MATERIALS
- Red Heart Super Saver medium (worsted) weight yarn (solid: 7 oz/ 364 yds/198g per skein; multi: 5 oz/244 yds/141g per skein):
  - 8 skeins #981 fall
  - 1 skein each #406 medium thyme and #378 claret

MEDIUM

- Size J/10/6mm crochet hook or size needed to obtain gauge

GAUGE
8 sc = 3 inches; 8 sc rows = 3 inches

SPECIAL STITCH
Cluster (cl): Yo, insert hook in indicted st, yo, pull lp through, yo, pull through 2 lps on hook, [yo, insert hook in same st, yo, pull lp through, yo, pull through 2 lps on hook] twice, yo, pull through all 4 lps on hook.

INSTRUCTIONS
AFGHAN
Row 1: With fall, ch 179, sc in 2nd ch from hook and in each of next 8 chs, *3 sc in next ch, sc in each of next 3 chs, sk next 2 chs, sc in each of next 3 chs, 3 sc in next ch, sc in each of next 9 chs**, sk next 2 chs, sc in each of next 9 chs, rep from * around, ending last rep at **, turn. (180 sc)

Rows 2–15: Ch 1, **sc dec** (see Stitch Guide) in first 2 sts, sc in each of next 8 sts, *3 sc in next

st, sc in each of next 3 sts, sk next 2 sts, sc in each of next 3 sts, 3 sc in next st**, sc in each of next 9 sts, sk next 2 sts, sc in each of next 9 sts, rep from * across, ending last rep at **, sc in each of next 8 sts, sc dec in last 2 sts, turn. Fasten off at end of last row.

Row 16: Join medium thyme with sl st in first st, ch 1, sc dec in first 2 sts, [**cl** (see Special Stitch) in next st, sc in each of next 2 sts] twice, cl in next st, sc in next st, *3 sc in next st, sc in next st, cl in next st, sc in next st, sk next 2 sts, sc in next st, cl in next st, sc in next st, 3 sc in next st, sc in next st, [cl in next st, sc in each of next 2 sts] twice, cl in next st**, sc in next st, sk next 2 sts, sc in next st [cl in next st, sc in each of next 2 sts] twice, cl in next st, sc in next st, rep from * across, ending last rep at **, sc dec in last 2 sts, turn. Fasten off. (180 sts)

Row 17: Join fall with sl st in first st, sc dec in first 2 sts, sc in each of next 8 sts, *3 sc in next st, sc in each of next 3 sts, sk next 2 sts, sc in each of next 3 sts, 3 sc in next st**, sc in each of next 9 sts, sk next 2 sts, sc in each of next 9 sts, rep from * across, ending last rep at **, sc in each of next 8 sts, sc dec in last 2 sts, turn.

Rows 18–31: Rep row 2. Fasten off at end of last row.

Row 32: With claret, rep row 16.

Row 33: Rep row 17.

Rows 34–47: Rep row 2.

Rows 48–111: [Rep rows 16–47 alternately] twice.

Rows 112–127: Rep rows 16–31. ∎

ASPEN Mile-a-Minute

SKILL LEVEL

INTERMEDIATE

FINISHED SIZE
44 x 57 inches

MATERIALS
- Red Heart Super Saver medium (worsted) weight yarn (solid: 7 oz/ 364 yds/198g per skein; multi: 5 oz/244 yds/141g per skein):
  - 6 skeins #305 aspen print
  - 3 skeins #336 warm brown
- Size I/9/5.5mm crochet hook or size needed to obtain gauge

GAUGE
11 dc = 4 inches

PATTERN NOTES
Join with slip stitch unless otherwise stated.

Chain-3 at beginning of rows counts as first double crochet unless otherwise stated.

SPECIAL STITCHES
Popcorn (pc): 4 dc in indicted place, drop lp from hook, insert hook in first dc of 4-dc group, pull dropped lp through.

Cluster (cl): Yo, insert hook in corresponding st on row 1 or in ch at base of corresponding sc on row 1, yo, pull lp through, yo, pull through 2 lps on hook, insert hook in next st on last row, yo, pull through all 3 lps on hook.

INSTRUCTIONS
STRIP
MAKE 10.
Row 1: With aspen print, ch 206, sc in 2nd ch from hook, [ch 2, sk next 2 chs, **pc** (see Special Stitches) in next ch, ch 2, sk next 2 chs, sc in next ch] across, **do not turn**. Fasten off. (68 ch sps, 35 sc, 34 pc)

Rnd 2: Now working in rnds, join warm brown in side of first st of first row, **ch 3** (see Pattern Notes), 4 dc in same row, 2 dc in each ch-2 sp across, 5 dc in opposite end of first row, working on opposite side of starting ch, 2 dc in each ch-2 sp across, join in 3rd ch of beg ch-3. Fasten off. (282 dc)

Rnd 3: Join aspen print with sc in first st, 2 sc in same st, sc in each of next 3 sts, 3 sc in next st, sc in each of next 4 sts, [**cl** (see Special Stitches), sc in each of next 3 sts] 33 times, 3 sc in next st, sc in each of next 3 sts, 3 sc in next st, sc in each of next 4 sts, [cl, sc in each of next 3 sts] 33 times, join in beg sc. (290 sc)

Rnd 4: Ch 3, 3 dc in next st, dc in each st around with 3 dc in center st of each 3-sc corner group, join in 3rd ch of beg ch-3. Fasten off. (298 dc)

Rnd 5: Join warm brown with sc in any st, sc in each st around with 3 sc in center st of each 3-sc corner group. (306 sc)

Holding 2 Strips long edges tog, join warm brown in 3rd st of 3-sc corner group after 1 short end on first Strip, ch 1, sl st in corresponding st on 2nd Strip, ch 1, sk next st on first st, sl st in next st, [ch 1, sk next st on 2nd Strip, sl st in next st, ch 1, sk next st on first st, sl st in next st] across with last st in center st of next 3-sc corner group on first Strip, ch 1, sl st in center st of next 3-sc corner group on 2nd Strip. Fasten off.

Join remaining Strips in same manner.

BORDER
Join aspen print in any st, ch 3, evenly sp dc around entire outer edge with 3 dc in each corner st, join in 3rd ch of beg ch-3. Fasten off. ∎

Desert
Miters

SKILL LEVEL

INTERMEDIATE

FINISHED SIZE
48 x 57 inches

MATERIALS
- Red Heart Super Saver medium (worsted) weight yarn (solid: 7 oz/ 364 yds/198g per skein; multi: 5 oz/244 yds/141g per skein):
  7 skeins #303 painted desert
  2 skeins #661 frosty green
- Size I/9/5.5mm crochet hook or size needed to obtain gauge
- Tapestry needle

GAUGE
11 sc = 4 inches; 13 sc rows = 4 inches; block = 6½ inches square

INSTRUCTIONS
BLOCK
MAKE 50.
Row 1: With painted desert, ch 36, sc in 2nd ch from hook and in each of next 15 chs, **sc dec** *(see Stitch Guide)* in first and 3rd of next 3 sts, sc in each of last 16 sts, turn. *(33 sc)*

Row 2: Ch 1, sc in each of first 15 sts, sc dec in first and 3rd of next 3 sts, sc in each of last 15 sts, turn. *(31 sc)*

Row 3: Ch 1, sc in each of first 14 sts, sc dec in first and 3rd of next 3 sts, sc in each of last 14 sts, turn. *(29 sc)*

Row 4: Ch 1, sc in each of first 13 sts, sc dec in first and 3rd of next 3 sts, sc in each of last 13 sts, turn. *(27 sc)*

Row 5: Ch 1, sc in each of first 12 sts, sc dec in first and 3rd of next 3 sts, sc in each of last 12 sts, turn. *(25 sc)*

Row 6: Ch 1, sc in each of first 11 sts, sc dec in first and 3rd of next 3 sts, sc in each of last 11 sts, turn. *(23 sc)*

Row 7: Ch 1, sc in each of first 10 sts, sc dec in first and 3rd of next 3 sts, sc in each of last 10 sts, turn. *(21 sc)*

Row 8: Ch 1, sc in each of first 9 sts, sc dec in first and 3rd of next 3 sts, sc in each of last 9 sts, turn. *(19 sc)*

Row 9: Ch 1, sc in each of first 8 sts, sc dec in first and 3rd of next 3 sts, sc in each of last 8 sts, turn. *(17 sc)*

Row 10: Ch 1, sc in each of first 7 sts, sc dec in first and 3rd of next 3 sts, sc in each of last 7 sts, turn. *(15 sc)*

Row 11: Ch 1, sc in each of first 6 sts, sc dec in first and 3rd of next 3 sts, sc in each of last 6 sts, turn. *(13 sc)*

Row 12: Ch 1, sc in each of first 5 sts, sc dec in first and 3rd of next 3 sts, sc in each of last 5 sts, turn. Fasten off. *(11 sc)*

Row 13: Join frosty green with sc in first st, sc in each of next 3 sts, sc dec in first and 3rd of next 3 sts, sc in each of last 4 sts, turn. *(9 sc)*

Row 14: Ch 1, sc in each of first 3 sts, sc dec in first and 3rd of next 3 sts, sc in each of last 3 sts, turn. *(7 sc)*

Row 15: Ch 1, sc in each of first 2 sts, sc dec in first and 3rd of next 3 sts, sc in each of last 2 sts, turn. *(5 sc)*

Row 16: Ch 1, sc first st, sc dec in first and 3rd of next 3 sts, sc in last st, turn. *(3 sc)*

Row 17: Ch 1, sc dec in first and last of next 3 sts, **do not turn**. *(1 sc)*

Rnd 18: Now working in rnds, ch 1, 3 sc in first st, evenly sp 15 sc across each side and 3 sc in each corner around, join with sl st in beg sc. Fasten off. *(72 sc)*

TRIANGLE
MAKE 10.

Row 1: With painted desert, ch 26, sc in 2nd ch from hook and in each ch across, turn. *(25 sc)*

Rows 2–12: Ch 1, sc dec in first 2 sts, sc in each st across to last 2 sts, sc dec in last 2 sts, turn. *(3 sc at end of last row)*

Row 13: Ch 1, sc dec in next 3 sts. Fasten off. *(1 sc)*

Rnd 14: Now working in rnds, join frosty green with sc in first st, 2 sc in same st, evenly sp 13 sc across each short side, 23 sc across long side and 3 sc in each corner, join with sl st in beg sc. Fasten off. *(58 sc)*

Holding Blocks and Triangles WS tog, working through **back lps** *(see Stitch Guide)*, sew tog according to Assembly Diagram.

BORDER

Join painted desert with sl st in center st of any 3-dc corner group, ch 3 *(counts as first dc)*, 4 dc in same st, dc in each st around with dc dec in next 5 sts in each indentation and 5 dc in center st of each 3-dc corner group, join with sl st in 3rd ch of beg ch-3. Fasten off. ∎

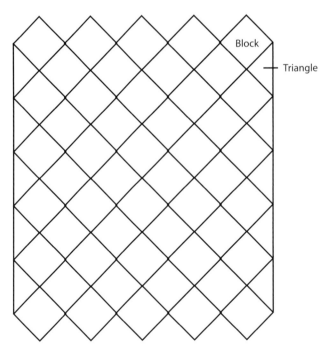

Desert Miters
Assembly Diagram

Stitch Guide

For more complete information, visit **FreePatterns.com**

ABBREVIATIONS

beg	begin/begins/beginning
bpdc	back post double crochet
bpsc	back post single crochet
bptr	back post treble crochet
CC	contrasting color
ch(s)	chain(s)
ch-	refers to chain or space previously made (e.g., ch-1 space)
ch sp(s)	chain space(s)
cl(s)	cluster(s)
cm	centimeter(s)
dc	double crochet (singular/plural)
dc dec	double crochet 2 or more stitches together, as indicated
dec	decrease/decreases/decreasing
dtr	double treble crochet
ext	extended
fpdc	front post double crochet
fpsc	front post single crochet
fptr	front post treble crochet
g	gram(s)
hdc	half double crochet
hdc dec	half double crochet 2 or more stitches together, as indicated
inc	increase/increases/increasing
lp(s)	loop(s)
MC	main color
mm	millimeter(s)
oz	ounce(s)
pc	popcorn(s)
rem	remain/remains/remaining
rep(s)	repeat(s)
rnd(s)	round(s)
RS	right side
sc	single crochet (singular/plural)
sc dec	single crochet 2 or more stitches together, as indicated
sk	skip/skipped/skipping
sl st(s)	slip stitch(es)
sp(s)	space/spaces/spaced
st(s)	stitch(es)
tog	together
tr	treble crochet
trtr	triple treble
WS	wrong side
yd(s)	yard(s)
yo	yarn over

Chain—ch: Yo, pull through lp on hook.

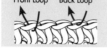

Slip stitch—sl st: Insert hook in st, pull through both lps on hook.

Single crochet—sc: Insert hook in st, yo, pull through st, yo, pull through both lps on hook.

Front post stitch—fp: Back post stitch—bp: When working post st, insert hook from right to left around post st on previous row.

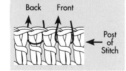

Front loop—front lp Back loop—back lp

Front Loop   Back Loop

Half double crochet— hdc: Yo, insert hook in st, yo, pull through st, yo, pull through all 3 lps on hook.

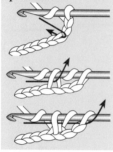

Double crochet—dc: Yo, insert hook in st, yo, pull through st, [yo, pull through 2 lps] twice.

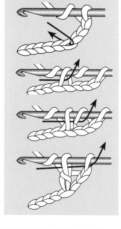

Change colors: Drop first color; with 2nd color, pull through last 2 lps of st.

Treble crochet—tr: Yo twice, insert hook in st, yo, pull through st, [yo, pull through 2 lps] 3 times.

Double treble crochet—dtr: Yo 3 times, insert hook in st, yo, pull through st, [yo, pull through 2 lps] 4 times.

Single crochet decrease (sc dec): (Insert hook, yo, draw lp through) in each of the sts indicated, yo, draw through all lps on hook.

Example of 2-sc dec

Half double crochet decrease (hdc dec): (Yo, insert hook, yo, draw lp through) in each of the sts indicated, yo, draw through all lps on hook.

Example of 2-hdc dec

Double crochet decrease (dc dec): (Yo, insert hook, yo, draw loop through, draw through 2 lps on hook) in each of the sts indicated, yo, draw through all lps on hook.

Example of 2-dc dec

Example of 2-tr dec

Treble crochet decrease (tr dec): Holding back last lp of each st, tr in each of the sts indicated, yo, pull through all lps on hook.

US		**UK**
sl st (slip stitch)	=	sc (single crochet)
sc (single crochet)	=	dc (double crochet)
hdc (half double crochet)	=	htr (half treble crochet)
dc (double crochet)	=	tr (treble crochet)
tr (treble crochet)	=	dtr (double treble crochet)
dtr (double treble crochet)	=	ttr (triple treble crochet)
skip	=	miss

Metric
Conversion
Charts

METRIC CONVERSIONS

yards	x	.9144	=	metres (m)
yards	x	91.44	=	centimetres (cm)
inches	x	2.54	=	centimetres (cm)
inches	x	25.40	=	millimetres (mm)
inches	x	.0254	=	metres (m)

centimetres	x	.3937	=	inches
metres	x	1.0936	=	yards

INCHES INTO MILLIMETRES & CENTIMETRES (Rounded off slightly)

inches	mm	cm	inches	cm	inches	cm	inches	cm
1/8	3	0.3	5	12.5	21	53.5	38	96.5
1/4	6	0.6	5 1/2	14	22	56	39	99
3/8	10	1	6	15	23	58.5	40	101.5
1/2	13	1.3	7	18	24	61	41	104
5/8	15	1.5	8	20.5	25	63.5	42	106.5
3/4	20	2	9	23	26	66	43	109
7/8	22	2.2	10	25.5	27	68.5	44	112
1	25	2.5	11	28	28	71	45	114.5
1 1/4	32	3.2	12	30.5	29	73.5	46	117
1 1/2	38	3.8	13	33	30	76	47	119.5
1 3/4	45	4.5	14	35.5	31	79	48	122
2	50	5	15	38	32	81.5	49	124.5
2 1/2	65	6.5	16	40.5	33	84	50	127
3	75	7.5	17	43	34	86.5		
3 1/2	90	9	18	46	35	89		
4	100	10	19	48.5	36	91.5		
4 1/2	115	11.5	20	51	37	94		

KNITTING NEEDLES CONVERSION CHART

Canada/U.S.	0	1	2	3	4	5	6	7	8	9	10	10½	11	13	15
Metric (mm)	2	2¼	2¾	3¼	3½	3¾	4	4½	5	5½	6	6½	8	9	10

CROCHET HOOKS CONVERSION CHART

Canada/U.S.	1/B	2/C	3/D	4/E	5/F	6/G	8/H	9/I	10/J	10½/K	N
Metric (mm)	2.25	2.75	3.25	3.5	3.75	4.25	5	5.5	6	6.5	9.0

Annie's Attic®

TOLL-FREE ORDER LINE or to request a free catalog (800) LV-ANNIE (800) 582-6643
Customer Service (800) AT-ANNIE (800) 282-6643, **Fax** (800) 882-6643
Visit AnniesAttic.com
We have made every effort to ensure the accuracy and completeness of these instructions.
We cannot, however, be responsible for human error, typographical mistakes or variations in individual work.

ISBN: 978-1-59635-250-6